JACKSONVILLE JAGUARS

ALL-TIME GREATS

BY TED COLEMAN

Book design by Jake Slavik
Cover design by Jake Slavik

Photographs ©: Terrance Williams/AP Images, cover (top), 1 (top); Gene J. Puskar/AP Images, cover (bottom), 1 (bottom); Focus on Sport/Getty Images Sport/Getty Images, 4; Andy Lyons/Allsport/Getty Images Sport/Getty Images, 6; Doug Benc/Getty Images Sport/Getty Images, 8, 10; John Capella/Sports Imagery/Getty Images Sport/Getty Images, 12; Michael DeHoog/Sports Imagery/Getty Images Sport/Getty Images, 14; Sam Greenwood/Getty Images Sport/Getty Images, 16, 18; Jeff Zelevansky/Getty Images Sport/Getty Images, 20

Press Box Books, an imprint of Press Room Editions.

ISBN
978-1-63494-428-1 (library bound)
978-1-63494-445-8 (paperback)
978-1-63494-478-6 (epub)
978-1-63494-462-5 (hosted ebook)

Library of Congress Control Number: 2021916600

Distributed by North Star Editions, Inc.
2297 Waters Drive
Mendota Heights, MN 55120
www.northstareditions.com

Printed in the United States of America
012022

ABOUT THE AUTHOR

Ted Coleman is a sportswriter who lives in Louisville, Kentucky, with his trusty Affenpinscher, Chloe.

TABLE OF CONTENTS

CHAPTER 1

EARLY SUCCESS 5

CHAPTER 2

GROWING PAINS 11

CHAPTER 3

LOOKING AHEAD 17

TIMELINE 22

TEAM FACTS 23

MORE INFORMATION 23

GLOSSARY 24

INDEX 24

BRUNELL
8

CHAPTER 1
EARLY SUCCESS

The Jacksonville Jaguars entered the National Football League (NFL) in 1995. Right away, the team had a good base for success. The Jaguars brought in three veteran quarterbacks. They were Steve Beuerlein, Andre Ware, and **Mark Brunell**. Brunell had been a backup with the Green Bay Packers. But he won the starting job in Jacksonville. Brunell made the most of his opportunity. He went on to set all the team's major passing records.

Jacksonville's first draft pick was offensive lineman **Tony Boselli**. For seven seasons, Boselli helped keep pass rushers out of Brunell's face. Boselli made the Pro Bowl in five of those years.

As Brunell improved, so did the Jaguars. Brunell had the help of wide receivers **Jimmy Smith** and **Keenan McCardell**. Together they were known as "Thunder and Lightning."

"Lightning" was Smith. The speedy receiver recorded his first 1,000-yard season in 1996. He went on to have eight more in his 11 years with the Jaguars. "Thunder" was McCardell. Over six seasons, McCardell racked up 6,393 receiving yards. He also scored 30 touchdowns. With "Thunder and Lightning," the Jaguars made a surprise run to the conference title game in the 1996 season. However, they fell to the New England Patriots.

COACH COUGHLIN

Head coach **Tom Coughlin** had more than two decades of experience when he took over the Jaguars in 1995. That made him a good choice to lead a new, young team. Coughlin was also Jacksonville's general manager. He was responsible for drafting and signing the team's players.

It was unusual for a new team to be good so early. The Jaguars got even better in 1998. That's when they drafted running back **Fred Taylor**. Taylor was a strong, powerful back.

He ran for more than 1,000 yards in seven of his 11 seasons with Jacksonville. Taylor dealt with many injuries during his career. Even so, he retired as one of the NFL's all-time leaders in rushing yards.

Defensive end **Tony Brackens** brought elite pass-rushing skills to the team. In 1999, Brackens recorded 12 sacks. The Jaguars had the league's best defense that year. And defense helped lead Jacksonville back to the conference title game. Unfortunately for Jaguars fans, the team lost to the Tennessee Titans.

STAT SPOTLIGHT

CAREER RUSHING YARDS

JAGUARS TEAM RECORD

Fred Taylor: 11,271

STROUD

99

CHAPTER 2
GROWING PAINS

The Jaguars kept Fred Taylor running wild into the 2000s. Offensive linemen **Brad Meester** and **Vince Manuwai** were big reasons why. Both played for Jacksonville their entire careers. Meester spent 14 years with the team. During that time, he rarely missed a game. Manuwai played eight seasons. He was one of the best run blockers in the NFL.

On the other side of the ball, defensive linemen **Marcus Stroud** and **John Henderson** formed their own dynamic duo. Stroud stood an impressive 6-foot-6. Henderson was even taller at 6-foot-7. For such

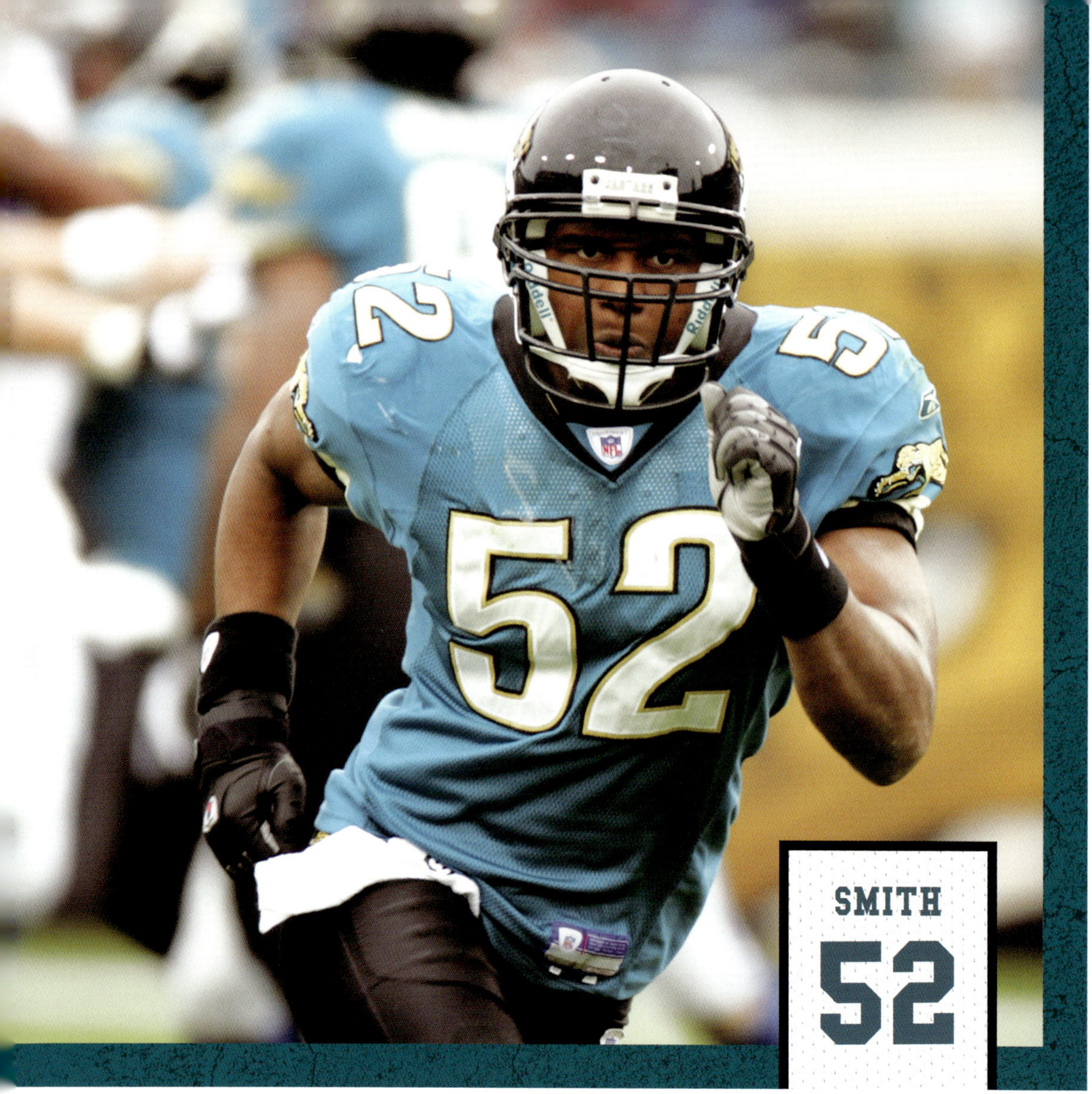

large men, both of them were quick. They were a nightmare for opposing teams to block.

Strong defenses helped Jacksonville stay competitive. The secondary was led by cornerback **Rashean Mathis**. Mathis created turnover after turnover in his 10 seasons with the Jaguars. He pulled down eight interceptions in 2006. That set a team record. Mathis had 30 picks during his time with Jacksonville. That was a team record, too.

At linebacker, **Daryl Smith** caused plenty of trouble for opposing runners. During Smith's nine years in Jacksonville, he made 540 tackles. Smith never reached the Pro Bowl. Even so, he quietly put together a rock-solid career. Teammates considered him one of the best linebackers in the game.

COACH DEL RIO

In the 1980s and 1990s, **Jack Del Rio** played linebacker in the NFL. And in 2003, he became Jacksonville's head coach. So, it wasn't surprising that the former linebacker focused on defense. In four of Del Rio's first five seasons, the Jaguars ranked among the top 10 in fewest points allowed.

The last three years of Taylor's Jaguars career were the first three for **Maurice Jones-Drew**. The duo formed a strong partnership. They rushed for a combined 5,437 yards during those years. When Taylor left the team, Jones-Drew proved he could handle things on his own. He used his speed and quick moves to gain 8,071 career rushing yards. That put him in second place behind Taylor on Jacksonville's all-time list.

The Jaguars drafted **David Garrard** in 2002. The team hoped it had found Mark Brunell's replacement. Garrard was a mobile quarterback. He was also known for his passing accuracy. Garrard led the Jaguars to a playoff win in 2007. However, he never quite lived up to his potential as the next franchise quarterback.

STAT SPOTLIGHT

CAREER RUSHING TOUCHDOWNS

JAGUARS TEAM RECORD

Maurice Jones-Drew: 68

BORTLES
5

CHAPTER 3
LOOKING AHEAD

The Jaguars' search for a franchise quarterback continued into the 2010s. **Blake Bortles** was the third overall draft pick in 2014. Bortles struggled as a rookie. But in 2015, he threw 35 touchdown passes. That was a team record. In five seasons with Jacksonville, Bortles had three of the best passing seasons in Jaguars history.

On defense, linebacker **Paul Posluszny** made a name for himself as a team leader. "Poz" was one of Jacksonville's most reliable players. He missed just 12 games in seven

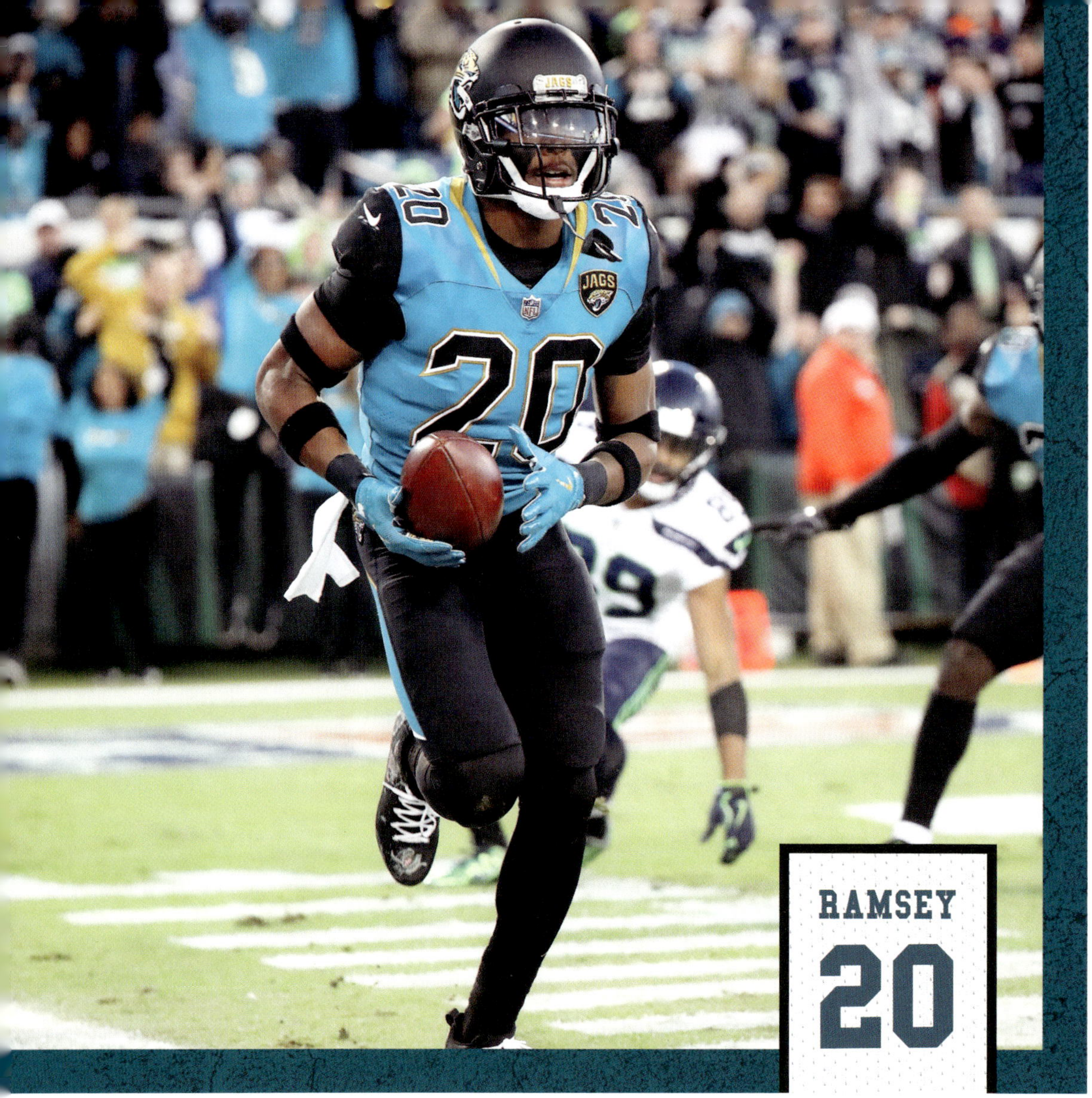

seasons. His 816 tackles were among the most in the NFL during that time.

Cornerback **Jalen Ramsey** was a leader in the secondary. Ramsey was a star as soon as he entered the league in 2016. He made his first Pro Bowl in 2017. That same year, the Jaguars had the league's best pass defense. Ramsey was an intense player with a talent for making interceptions. But he didn't stay in Jacksonville for long. The team traded him to the Los Angeles Rams in 2019.

Defensive end **Calais Campbell** was near the end of a great career when he signed with Jacksonville in 2017. Campbell proved he still had what it took to play at a high level. He had a career-high 14.5 sacks that season. That was a new team record.

SACKSONVILLE

The Jaguars defense started out the 2017 season with a bang. They racked up 10 sacks in their first game. The nickname "Sacksonville" was born. Calais Campbell led the team in sacks that year. The mayor of Jacksonville even gave Campbell a new title. Campbell became known as the "Mayor of Sacksonville."

JACK
44

Campbell served as a mentor to defensive end **Josh Allen**. Allen was a rookie in 2019. Right away, he showed a natural talent for rushing the passer. He recorded 10.5 sacks that year. He also made the Pro Bowl.

Posluszny retired after the 2017 season. He left the defense in good hands, though. Linebacker **Myles Jack** had a quiet rookie season in 2016. But he kept improving. By 2020, he was among the league leaders in tackles. Jack could make plays from just about anywhere on the field.

In 2021, quarterback **Trevor Lawrence** joined the Jaguars. He was the top pick in that year's draft. Lawrence had been one of the best quarterbacks in college football. Jaguars fans hoped he could become one of the best in the NFL.

TIMELINE

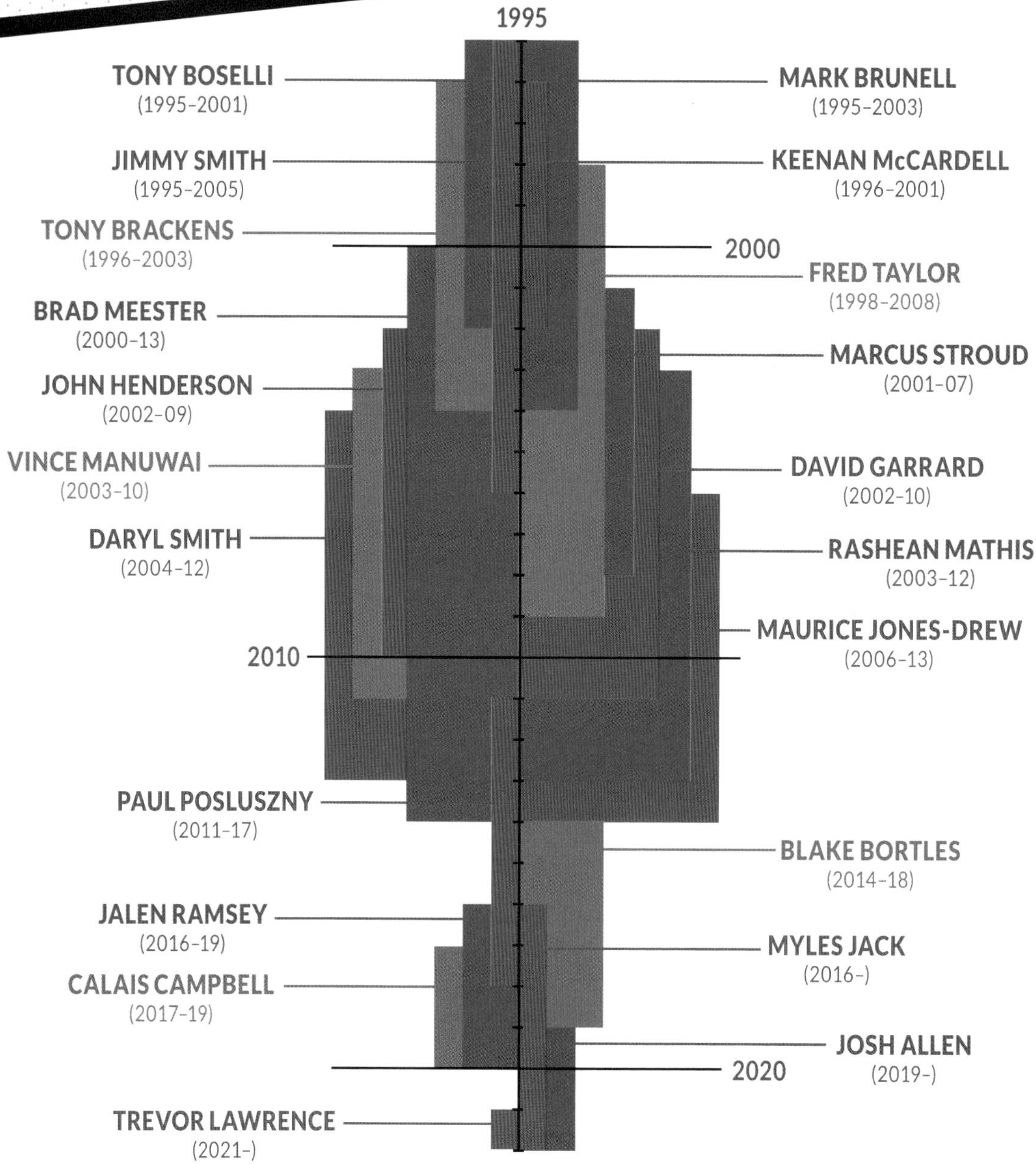
1995
TONY BOSELLI
(1995–2001)
MARK BRUNELL
(1995–2003)
JIMMY SMITH
(1995–2005)
KEENAN McCARDELL
(1996–2001)
TONY BRACKENS
(1996–2003)
2000
FRED TAYLOR
(1998–2008)
BRAD MEESTER
(2000–13)
MARCUS STROUD
(2001–07)
JOHN HENDERSON
(2002–09)
VINCE MANUWAI
(2003–10)
DAVID GARRARD
(2002–10)
DARYL SMITH
(2004–12)
RASHEAN MATHIS
(2003–12)
MAURICE JONES-DREW
(2006–13)
2010
PAUL POSLUSZNY
(2011–17)
BLAKE BORTLES
(2014–18)
JALEN RAMSEY
(2016–19)
MYLES JACK
(2016–)
CALAIS CAMPBELL
(2017–19)
JOSH ALLEN
(2019–)
2020
TREVOR LAWRENCE
(2021–)

TEAM FACTS

JACKSONVILLE JAGUARS

Founded: 1995

Super Bowl titles: 0*

Key coaches:

Tom Coughlin (1995–2002), 68–60–0

Jack Del Rio (2003–11), 68–71–0

MORE INFORMATION

To learn more about the Jacksonville Jaguars, go to **pressboxbooks.com/AllAccess**.

These links are routinely monitored and updated to provide the most current information available.

**1966 through 2020*

GLOSSARY

conference
A subset of teams within a sports league.

draft
An event that allows teams to choose new players coming into the league.

franchise quarterback
A quarterback capable of leading a team for a number of years.

offensive linemen
Players who stop defenders from reaching the quarterback and block for running backs.

Pro Bowl
The NFL's all-star game, in which the league's best players compete.

rookie
A professional athlete in his or her first year of competition.

secondary
The defensive players who typically cover wide receivers.

veteran
A player who has spent several years in a league.

INDEX

Allen, Josh, 21

Bortles, Blake, 17
Boselli, Tony, 6
Brackens, Tony, 9
Brunell, Mark, 5–7, 15

Campbell, Calais, 19, 21

Garrard, David, 15

Henderson, John, 11–12

Jack, Myles, 21
Jones-Drew, Maurice, 14–15

Lawrence, Trevor, 21

Manuwai, Vince, 11
Mathis, Rashean, 13
McCardell, Keenan, 7
Meester, Brad, 11

Posluszny, Paul, 17–18, 21

Ramsey, Jalen, 18–19

Smith, Daryl, 13
Smith, Jimmy, 7
Stroud, Marcus, 11–12

Taylor, Fred, 8–9, 11, 14–15